Salahddine KRIT

AI Tools and Applications

Salahddine KRIT

AI Tools and Applications

A Free Practical Guide for Students, Developers, and Researchers

Noor Publishing

Imprint
Any brand names and product names mentioned in this book are subject to trademark, brand or patent protection and are trademarks or registered trademarks of their respective holders. The use of brand names, product names, common names, trade names, product descriptions etc. even without a particular marking in this work is in no way to be construed to mean that such names may be regarded as unrestricted in respect of trademark and brand protection legislation and could thus be used by anyone.

Cover image: www.ingimage.com

Publisher:
Noor Publishing
is a trademark of
Dodo Books Indian Ocean Ltd. and OmniScriptum S.R.L publishing group

120 High Road, East Finchley, London, N2 9ED, United Kingdom
Str. Armeneasca 28/1, office 1, Chisinau MD-2012, Republic of Moldova, Europe
Managing Directors: Ieva Konstantinova, Victoria Ursu
info@omniscriptum.com

Printed at: see last page
ISBN: 978-620-0-04788-5

AI Tools and Applications

A Free Practical Guide for Students, Developers, and Researchers

Author : Dr. Salahddine Krit

Table of Contents

Preface

As an educator, researcher, and technology enthusiast, I have witnessed firsthand how artificial intelligence is transforming not only industries but also the everyday lives of students, developers, and professionals around the world.

This guide was born from a simple realization: **many powerful AI tools are available for free**, yet remain largely unknown or underutilized by those who could benefit most. My goal is to bridge that gap — to provide a **clear, structured, and accessible resource** that helps you discover, evaluate, and apply the best AI tools currently available, without the noise or confusion that often comes with fast-moving technologies.

Whether you are conducting academic research, building a prototype, automating workflows, or exploring digital creativity, this guide is for you. It is **not a technical manual**, but rather a **practical roadmap** — one that highlights possibilities and empowers action.

As AI continues to evolve, I believe that **democratizing access** to these tools is not only beneficial, but essential. This guide is a small contribution to that mission.

I hope it helps you learn, build, and create with confidence.

— Dr. Salah-ddine Krit
Professor, Engineer, and AI Practitioner

General Introduction

Artificial Intelligence (AI) is no longer a distant promise—it's an integral part of modern technological ecosystems. From natural language processing and generative design to autonomous agents and intelligent automation, AI has evolved into a **powerful, accessible set of tools** that empower individuals as much as enterprises.

This eBook is crafted as a **practical and curated guide** to the most relevant **free and freemium AI tools available as of 2025**, specifically tailored for **students, developers, and researchers**. Whether you're writing a thesis, prototyping an app, automating repetitive workflows, or exploring multimodal creativity, you'll find tools in this guide that can accelerate your journey — without requiring deep expertise in data science or machine learning.

□ Why This Matters — From Theory to Practice

While academic courses often focus on the *foundations* of AI — algorithms, models, and ethics — the actual *practice* of using AI in real-world scenarios can be elusive. This guide fills that gap by introducing a wide spectrum of tools that leverage:

- **Transformer-based models** (e.g., GPT, Claude, Gemini),
- **Stable Diffusion and GANs** for image generation,
- **Autonomous task agents** capable of multi-step reasoning,
- **Low-code/no-code interfaces** that reduce technical barriers.

The included platforms have been selected not only for their **technical robustness** but also for their **user accessibility**, community support, and real-world relevance. These tools allow users to:

- Write and debug code collaboratively with AI copilots,
- Summarize, annotate, and map academic literature,
- Build full-stack applications using prompt-based logic,
- Generate music, video, and visual assets for games or apps,
- Deploy AI agents that act independently toward user-defined goals.

□ Who Is This Guide For?

- **Students** who want to enhance their research, automate tasks, or build AI-powered projects with minimal cost and setup.
- **Developers** looking for AI-enhanced workflows, from intelligent IDEs to autonomous coding agents.
- **Researchers** who seek to optimize literature reviews, test experimental ideas, or stay up to date with state-of-the-art capabilities.

You don't need to be a data scientist to benefit from this book — but by the time you finish it, you may start thinking like one.

□ **What You'll Find Inside**

The guide is organized by **domain of application**:

- Research assistants, academic tools, and citation-aware AI
- Productivity and task automation agents
- Code generation, debugging, and versioning aids
- Game and app development platforms (no-code/low-code)
- Art, design, and multimedia generation systems
- Open-source playgrounds for experimentation

Each tool is presented with:

- A **brief technical description**,
- Core **features and limitations**,
- A **direct link** for hands-on testing,
- Tags to help you filter by use-case (e.g., text, image, audio, web, mobile, etc.).

In an era where **AI is both a creative partner and a computational engine**, knowing the right tools is as valuable as knowing the right techniques. This book is your field guide to both.

Chapter I. AI and Free Tools Landscape

□ **Why Use AI Tools?**

Artificial Intelligence (AI) has transitioned from a niche discipline into a mainstream, cross-disciplinary force, reshaping industries from healthcare to education, software development, art, and research. AI tools now offer capabilities that can:

- **Boost productivity** by automating repetitive or complex tasks
- **Enhance creativity** through generative design, writing, coding, or art
- **Accelerate research** with smart literature reviews, data analysis, and summarization
- **Enable innovation** by making advanced capabilities accessible without the need for specialized technical skills

Whether you're a student working on a final-year project, a developer building an app, or a researcher analyzing data, AI tools allow you to **work smarter, faster, and with fewer resources**.

Importantly, the rise of **user-friendly, no-code platforms** has removed many of the traditional barriers to entry. You no longer need to be a machine learning expert to take advantage of powerful AI features — and many of the most useful tools are **completely free or offer generous free tiers**.

What Is "Freemium"?

The term **freemium** refers to a business model where software is **free to use with optional paid upgrades**. In the AI ecosystem, this means you can often:

- Access core features at no cost
- Use the platform for personal, academic, or non-commercial work
- Upgrade to paid plans only when you need advanced features (e.g., more credits, commercial licenses, API access)

Examples of freemium models in AI tools:

- **ChatGPT**: free to use with GPT-3.5; paid access unlocks GPT-4 and advanced tools
- **Leonardo.Ai**: daily free image generation credits, with premium options for faster or unlimited usage
- **Taskade**: basic AI task manager features for free; premium collaboration tools available as upgrades

For learners and innovators, the freemium model is a powerful gateway: it enables **experimentation and exploration without financial risk**.

Overview of Application Categories

This guide classifies AI tools into **eight practical domains**, designed to meet the everyday needs of students, researchers, and developers. Here's a preview of what each category includes:

Category	**What You Can Do**
Research Assistants	Automate literature reviews, extract summaries, generate citations
Personal Productivity	Plan, take notes, organize tasks, and think with an AI partner
Automation Agents	Build workflows or autonomous agents that complete tasks for you
Coding & Development	Generate, autocomplete, debug, and deploy code using AI
App & Game Creation	Build full applications and games with no-code or low-code AI
Design & Multimedia	Generate art, images, logos, slides, videos, and music
Worldbuilding & Assets	Create 2D/3D environments, NPCs, quests, dialogue, or soundtracks
Experimental Tools	Explore open-source or cutting-edge AI platforms for advanced use

table 1 : eight practical domains

Each section in this book will introduce a curated set of tools under these domains — each chosen for its **usability, performance, and real-world relevance** in academic or creative workflows.

Chapter.2 AI for Learning and Research

AI is transforming the academic landscape by offering tools that assist with **literature reviews**, **research organization**, **knowledge discovery**, and **scientific writing**. For students, educators, and researchers, these tools can reduce time spent on manual research and increase the quality of academic output.

Below is a categorized list of **free or freemium AI platforms** designed specifically to support research and academic tasks.

□ Key AI Tools for Academic Research

Tool	Function	Use Case	Link
Elicit	Literature rcview assistant	Generate summaries, extract key findings from academic papers based on research questions	elicit.org
Perplexity AI	Conversational research engine	Find real-time answers with references and citations	perplexity.ai
Consensus	Scientific question answering	Summarize what peer-reviewed papers say about a research query	consensus.app
Scite Assistant	Contextual citation explorer	Understand how a paper was cited and its scientific credibility	scite.ai
ResearchRabbit	Citation network explorer	Discover new papers and visualize research relationships	researchrabbit.ai

table 2 : AI Tools for Academic Research

□ Additional Free AI Tools for Learning and Knowledge Building

Tool	Function	Use Case	Link
ChatGPT Free	General-purpose assistant	Summarize, brainstorm, explain complex topics	chat.openai.com
Claude.ai (free)	Conversational AI with strong reasoning	Analyze documents and extract structured knowledge	claude.ai
PI by Inflection AI	Personal and reflective AI	Help with planning, reflection, idea	pi.ai

		generation	
ClassCentral	Free certified courses	Learn AI, machine learning, and academic research skills	classcentral.com
Notion AI (limited free)	AI writing inside a workspace	Draft, summarize, brainstorm notes and research plans	notion.so
Mem.ai	Smart note-taking with AI	Organize and retrieve notes, research memos, and drafts	mem.ai
Taskade AI	Productivity and learning workspace	Plan research tasks, write outlines, mindmap content	taskade.com
EaseMate	Multi-model research assistant	Query multiple LLMs (GPT, Claude, Gemini) for varied perspectives	easemate.io
Emergent App	AI co-pilot for knowledge synthesis	Use multiple AI agents for note structuring and learning	emergentapp.ai

table 3 : AI Tools for Learning and Knowledge Building

□ **Practical Use Cases**

□ **Students**

- Use Elicit and Perplexity to gather sources quickly
- Draft essay outlines or summaries using ChatGPT or Claude
- Use Notion AI to manage study notes and project deadlines

□ **Researchers**

- Map publication networks with ResearchRabbit
- Evaluate citation credibility with Scite
- Use Consensus to get fast answers backed by literature

□ **Educators**

- Use ClassCentral to share certified AI learning paths
- Recommend task planning with Taskade AI or Mem.ai
- Use Claude or GPT to generate study materials

□ Tips for Using AI in Academia

- Always **verify AI-generated outputs**, especially citations or factual claims.
- Use AI tools as **assistants, not authorities** — they help you think faster, not replace thinking.
- Combine tools: e.g., ask Perplexity to generate a draft, validate it with Scite, and organize notes in Notion.

Chapter 3: AI for Productivity and Personal Use

In today's fast-paced world, managing tasks, notes, ideas, and communication efficiently is crucial. Artificial Intelligence (AI) tools have become indispensable for enhancing productivity by automating routine tasks, organizing information intelligently, and even providing emotional support. This chapter explores some of the best AI-powered applications designed to help individuals and professionals boost their productivity and streamline daily workflows.

3.1 Introduction

AI for productivity focuses on simplifying complex tasks, reducing cognitive load, and increasing efficiency through smart automation. Unlike AI designed for specialized domains such as healthcare or finance, productivity AIs are general-purpose assistants or workspace enhancers that adapt to user behavior and context.

We will review popular AI tools in this domain:

- Pi by Inflection AI
- ChatGPT Free
- Notion AI (limited free version)
- Mem.ai
- Taskade AI

Each tool offers unique features tailored to different aspects of productivity, from emotional support to note-taking and task management.

3.2 Pi (Inflection AI): Your Emotional AI Assistant

Website: https://pi.ai

Pi is an AI assistant designed to engage users in emotionally intelligent conversations. Beyond answering queries, Pi emphasizes empathy, companionship, and emotional well-being. This makes it ideal for users seeking not only productivity help but also conversational support.

Key Features

- Natural language conversations with emotional awareness
- Personal journaling and reflective prompts
- Context retention for meaningful interactions
- Support for motivation and mood tracking

Use Cases

- Managing stress and improving mental health
- Brainstorming ideas with an empathetic AI partner
- Casual chat to break monotony and recharge focus

3.3 ChatGPT Free: The Versatile AI Assistant

Website: https://chat.openai.com

ChatGPT is a state-of-the-art language model by OpenAI, capable of understanding and generating human-like text. The free version offers broad versatility for tasks including writing, brainstorming, coding help, and general Q&A.

Key Features

- Generate and refine text content (emails, reports, summaries)
- Answer complex questions instantly
- Help with creative writing and problem-solving
- Integration with various apps via API (advanced use)

Use Cases

- Drafting documents, emails, and social media posts
- Learning new topics or summarizing research
- Programming support and debugging
- Personalized tutoring and study assistance

3.4 Notion AI (Limited Free Version): AI Inside Your Workspace

Website: https://notion.so

Notion is a popular all-in-one workspace app for notes, documents, databases, and project management. Its AI feature helps users create, edit, and organize content faster by generating summaries, rewriting text, and brainstorming ideas within the workspace.

Key Features

- AI writing assistance embedded directly in notes
- Summarization and content generation
- Task and project management integration
- Collaboration with teams in real time

Use Cases

- Creating meeting notes and project plans
- Automating repetitive writing tasks
- Enhancing team collaboration through shared AI assistance

3.5 Mem.ai: Smart AI Note-Taking and Knowledge Management

Website: https://mem.ai

Mem.ai leverages AI to transform note-taking from a passive activity into an active knowledge-building process. It automatically organizes notes, links related ideas, and reminds you of important information when you need it.

Key Features

- AI-powered content capture and organization
- Smart linking of notes and ideas
- Contextual reminders and memory triggers
- Natural language search and retrieval

Use Cases

- Personal knowledge management for lifelong learning
- Preparing research and study materials
- Organizing meeting notes with automatic tagging

3.6 Taskade AI: Task Management and Mind Mapping

Website: https://taskade.com

Taskade combines task lists, notes, and mind maps into a unified platform enhanced by AI. It helps users plan projects, brainstorm ideas visually, and track progress with smart suggestions and templates.

Key Features

- AI-assisted task creation and prioritization
- Visual mind mapping for idea organization
- Real-time collaboration with teammates
- Customizable templates and workflows

Use Cases

- Project planning and agile task management
- Brainstorming sessions with visual maps
- Coordinating team projects and deadlines

3.7 Summary Table of AI Productivity Tools

Tool	Description	Website
Pi (Inflection AI)	Emotional AI assistant	pi.ai
ChatGPT Free	General-purpose AI assistant	chat.openai.com
Notion AI (limited free)	AI inside Notion workspace	notion.so
Mem.ai	Smart AI note-taking and knowledge mgmt	mem.ai
Taskade AI	Task management & mind maps	taskade.com

table 4 : AI Productivity Tools

3.8 How to Get Started

1. **Identify your productivity needs:** Are you focused on note-taking, emotional support, task management, or general assistance?
2. **Try free versions:** Most tools offer free tiers—explore their features without cost.
3. **Experiment with workflows:** Integrate the AI into daily routines gradually, such as journaling with Pi or managing projects with Taskade.
4. **Scale with paid features:** If useful, consider upgrading to unlock advanced capabilities and integrations.

3.9 Future Outlook

AI productivity tools continue to evolve rapidly, incorporating deeper contextual understanding, multimodal inputs (voice, images), and stronger integrations with popular platforms. Staying updated with emerging tools will help you maintain a productivity edge in personal and professional spheres.

Chapter 4: Autonomous Agents and Task Automation

In the evolving landscape of Artificial Intelligence, autonomous agents and task automation represent a leap toward AI systems capable of independently performing complex workflows with minimal human intervention. These technologies promise to revolutionize productivity by automating repetitive tasks, managing workflows across apps, and executing multi-step goals intelligently.

This chapter explores some of the most powerful AI tools and frameworks designed to create, manage, and deploy autonomous agents that streamline tasks and workflows.

4.1 Introduction

Autonomous agents are AI-driven software entities that can perceive their environment, make decisions, and take actions to achieve specific objectives without continuous human guidance. Paired with task automation platforms, they enable users to offload routine and complex workflows, freeing up time and increasing efficiency.

We will review five leading tools in this domain:

- AgentGPT
- Auto-GPT
- BabyAGI
- Runner AI
- Zapier AI

These tools range from open-source frameworks to no-code platforms, each providing unique capabilities for task automation and autonomous agent creation.

4.2 AgentGPT: Create Autonomous Agents Easily

Website: https://agentgpt.reworkd.ai

AgentGPT is a user-friendly web platform that allows anyone to create AI-powered autonomous agents tailored to perform a variety of tasks. It offers an intuitive interface to design, test, and deploy agents without requiring programming skills.

Key Features

- Visual agent creation and management
- Customizable goals and task flows

- Integration with external APIs and services
- Real-time monitoring of agent activities

Use Cases

- Automating customer support workflows
- Data collection and analysis
- Personal productivity assistants

4.3 Auto-GPT: Python-Based Autonomous Agent Framework

Repository: https://github.com/Significant-Gravitas/Auto-GPT

Auto-GPT is an open-source Python application that leverages GPT-4 to create fully autonomous agents capable of performing multi-step tasks. It's designed for developers and enthusiasts who want to experiment with cutting-edge AI automation.

Key Features

- Recursive task execution using GPT-4
- Autonomous goal setting and planning
- Plugin support for expanded functionality
- Configurable memory and resource management

Use Cases

- Research automation
- Personal task automation
- Prototype AI projects requiring multi-step reasoning

4.4 BabyAGI: Task Queue AI Agent

Repository: https://github.com/yoheinakajima/babyagi

BabyAGI is an open-source project that builds on concepts from Auto-GPT to create an AI agent that manages tasks using a queue system. It can generate, prioritize, and execute tasks autonomously based on defined goals.

Key Features

- Task queue management and prioritization
- Autonomous task generation based on results
- Simple, modular Python codebase for customization

Use Cases

- Project management automation
- Research task orchestration
- Experimenting with AI task decomposition

4.5 Runner AI: No-Code AI Automation Platform

Website: https://runner.hcompany.ai

Runner AI is a no-code platform designed for business users to create AI-driven automation workflows without programming knowledge. It enables building complex automation pipelines integrating AI capabilities.

Key Features

- Drag-and-drop workflow builder
- Integration with multiple apps and data sources
- AI-powered decision-making nodes
- Scalable automation pipelines

Use Cases

- Automating marketing campaigns
- Sales workflow automation
- Customer engagement and support automation

4.6 Zapier AI: Automate App Workflows with AI

Website: https://zapier.com/ai

Zapier AI extends the popular Zapier automation platform by incorporating AI functionalities. Users can automate workflows across thousands of apps with AI-powered triggers, actions, and data transformations.

Key Features

- Connects 5000+ apps for workflow automation
- AI-powered triggers and dynamic content generation
- No-code interface for easy automation setup
- Custom AI models integration

Use Cases

- Automating repetitive data entry

- Dynamic email and content generation
- Cross-app workflow synchronization

4.7 Summary Table of Autonomous Agents and Task Automation Tools

Tool	Description	Link
AgentGPT	Create autonomous agents easily	agentgpt.reworkd.ai
Auto-GPT	Python-based autonomous agent	github.com/Significant-Gravitas/Auto-GPT
BabyAGI	Task queue AI agent	github.com/yoheinakajima/babyagi
Runner AI	No-code AI automation platform	runner.hcompany.ai
Zapier AI	Automate app workflows with AI	zapier.com/ai

table 5 : Autonomous Agents and Task Automation Tools

4.8 How to Get Started

1. **Define your automation goals:** Identify the tasks or workflows you want to automate and whether you prefer code-based or no-code solutions.
2. **Explore the platforms:** Try AgentGPT or Runner AI for easy entry; dive into Auto-GPT or BabyAGI if you have programming skills and want more customization.
3. **Prototype small projects:** Build simple agents or workflows to understand the tool's capabilities before scaling.
4. **Integrate with your tools:** Connect your AI agents to apps and services you already use to maximize productivity gains.
5. **Monitor and iterate:** Autonomous agents can be unpredictable; regular monitoring and fine-tuning improve their performance and reliability.

4.9 Future Outlook

The field of autonomous agents and task automation is rapidly growing, driven by advances in large language models and integration technologies. We expect smarter, more adaptable agents capable of complex decision-making and seamless interaction across diverse systems. Keeping abreast of this space will empower users and organizations to unlock new productivity frontiers.

4.10 Getting Started Tutorials

4.10.1 AgentGPT: Quick Start Guide

1. Visit agentgpt.reworkd.ai and sign up for a free account.
2. Click **Create New Agent** and choose a name and goal for your agent.
3. Customize the agent's personality or skillset by selecting predefined tasks or inputting specific instructions.
4. Connect external APIs if needed to enable agent interactions with other services (e.g., Google Sheets, email).
5. Launch your agent and monitor its activity dashboard to review task progress and outputs.
6. Adjust parameters or goals as needed to refine agent behavior.

AgentGPT is ideal for non-programmers looking for quick deployment of autonomous agents.

4.10.2 Auto-GPT: Basic Setup and Usage

1. Access the repository at github.com/Significant-Gravitas/Auto-GPT.
2. Follow the README to clone the repo and install dependencies using Python (requires Python 3.8+).
3. Obtain OpenAI API keys and set up environment variables as instructed.
4. Define the goal for your autonomous agent in the configuration files.
5. Run the Auto-GPT script and observe the agent executing tasks, generating sub-tasks, and iterating autonomously.
6. Customize memory, task limits, and plugins as your project grows.

Auto-GPT is suited for developers comfortable with Python who want powerful, fully autonomous AI agents.

4.10.3 BabyAGI: Running the Task Queue Agent

1. Visit github.com/yoheinakajima/babyagi and clone the repository.
2. Install dependencies and configure your OpenAI API key.
3. Modify the initial objective and task queue parameters in the script.
4. Run the Python script to see BabyAGI autonomously generate and prioritize tasks to achieve the goal.
5. Monitor logs for task creation and completion status.

BabyAGI is great for experimenting with task management and AI-driven project orchestration.

4.10.4 Runner AI: No-Code Automation Workflow

1. Go to runner.hcompany.ai and create a free account.
2. Use the drag-and-drop interface to build workflows by adding triggers, AI-powered decision nodes, and actions.
3. Connect apps like Slack, Gmail, or CRM tools through built-in integrations.
4. Test the workflow with sample data to ensure correct automation behavior.
5. Activate the workflow and monitor performance via the dashboard.

Runner AI fits business users and marketers who want AI automation without coding.

4.10.5 Zapier AI: Automate with AI in Your Apps

1. Sign up or log in at zapier.com/ai.
2. Create a new Zap (automation) and select a trigger app and event.
3. Add an AI-powered action, such as text generation, summarization, or sentiment analysis.
4. Map data fields from the trigger to the AI action inputs.
5. Add additional steps or conditions to complete the workflow.
6. Test and enable your Zap to run automatically.

Zapier AI is perfect for anyone wanting to automate multi-app workflows enhanced with AI capabilities.

4.11 Comparison Matrix: Pros, Cons, and Ideal Users

Tool	Pros	Cons	Ideal Users
AgentGPT	Easy agent creation without coding; real-time monitoring	Limited to web interface; fewer customization options	Non-programmers; small business owners
Auto-GPT	Highly flexible and powerful; open-source; plugin support	Requires programming skills; complex setup	Developers, AI researchers, hobbyists
BabyAGI	Simple codebase; effective task queue management	Still experimental; less user-friendly	Developers experimenting with AI workflows
Runner	No-code drag-and-	Limited to available	Business users,

AI	drop; integrates many apps	integrations; paid plans for advanced features	marketers, operations teams
Zapier AI	Supports thousands of apps; AI-enhanced actions	AI features are relatively new; pricing tiers apply	General users needing cross-app automation

table 6 : Matrix: Pros, Cons, and Ideal Users

4.12 Sample Project Ideas

AgentGPT

- **Customer FAQ Bot:** Build an agent that autonomously answers common customer questions on your website, escalating complex queries to human staff.
- **Personal Research Assistant:** Create an agent to gather and summarize news articles on a chosen topic daily.

Auto-GPT

- **Automated Content Creation:** Set a goal for the agent to research, draft, and edit blog posts on tech trends without manual intervention.
- **Email Management Agent:** Automate reading, categorizing, and replying to routine emails using natural language.

BabyAGI

- **Project Task Manager:** Use BabyAGI to break down a large project into manageable tasks, prioritize, and track completion automatically.
- **Market Analysis Pipeline:** Automate collection and analysis of stock market data, triggering alerts for actionable insights.

Runner AI

- **Marketing Campaign Workflow:** Automate lead capturing, email follow-ups, and social media posting in a single drag-and-drop pipeline.
- **HR Onboarding Process:** Streamline candidate screening, interview scheduling, and documentation using automated workflows.

Zapier AI

- **Dynamic Social Media Posts:** Automate creation and posting of social media updates triggered by new blog content, enhanced with AI-generated hashtags.
- **Customer Feedback Analysis:** Collect survey responses and use AI to summarize sentiment and key themes automatically.

4.13 Template Workflows and Example Code Snippets

AgentGPT Example Workflow

- **Goal:** Automate daily news briefing
- Steps:
    1. Agent searches news APIs for headlines on chosen topics.
    2. Summarizes each article with AI.
    3. Emails compiled briefing to user.

Auto-GPT Minimal Python Example

python
CopyEdit
```
from auto_gpt import AutoGPT

agent = AutoGPT(openai_api_key='your-api-key',
  goals=["Research and write a summary about renewable energy innovations."])
agent.start()
```

BabyAGI Basic Task Queue (Python snippet)

python
CopyEdit
```
tasks = ["Collect recent AI papers", "Summarize key findings", "Prepare presentation slides"]

for task in tasks:
  print(f"Executing task: {task}")
  # Add task execution logic here
```

Runner AI Simple No-Code Workflow

- Trigger: New CRM lead created
- Action 1: AI scores lead quality
- Action 2: If score > threshold, send personalized email
- Action 3: Create follow-up task in task manager

Zapier AI Workflow Example

- Trigger: New form submission
- Action: Use AI to analyze sentiment of response
- Action: Send alert email if negative sentiment detected

4.14 Best Practices for Safe and Effective Autonomous Agents

1. **Define Clear Objectives:** Set well-scoped, measurable goals for your agents to prevent unintended behaviors.
2. **Start Small and Monitor:** Begin with limited tasks and closely monitor agent outputs before scaling.
3. **Use Rate Limits and Safeguards:** Implement API rate limits and error handling to avoid runaway executions.
4. **Keep Human-in-the-Loop:** Design workflows to allow human review or override when necessary.
5. **Secure API Keys and Data:** Store credentials securely and comply with privacy regulations when handling user data.
6. **Regularly Update and Maintain:** Keep your agent frameworks and integrations up to date to avoid security and performance issues.
7. **Test Thoroughly:** Test agents in sandbox environments to catch bugs or unexpected results early.
8. **Document Workflows:** Maintain clear documentation for your agents' purpose, configuration, and limits.

Chapter 5: AI for Coding and Development

The world of software development is rapidly evolving with the integration of Artificial Intelligence, transforming how developers write, debug, and optimize code. AI-powered coding assistants and IDEs accelerate productivity, reduce errors, and help both beginners and experts by suggesting code completions, generating snippets, and automating repetitive tasks.

This chapter explores the leading AI tools designed to enhance coding and development workflows, empowering developers to build software faster and more efficiently.

5.1 Introduction

AI for coding leverages large language models and domain-specific training to understand programming languages, APIs, and developer intent. These tools assist with:

- Code completion and suggestions
- Automated code generation
- Real-time error detection and debugging
- Code execution and testing
- Enhancing collaboration in cloud IDEs

We will cover five popular AI coding tools:

- GitHub Copilot
- Codeium
- OpenDevin
- Cursor
- Replit Ghostwriter

5.2 GitHub Copilot: AI Code Completion (Free for Students)

Website: https://github.com/features/copilot

GitHub Copilot, powered by OpenAI Codex, is one of the most widely adopted AI code completion tools. Integrated into editors like VS Code, it predicts and generates code snippets based on the context, significantly speeding up coding.

Key Features

- Context-aware code suggestions
- Support for multiple programming languages
- In-line documentation generation
- Free for verified students and educators

Use Cases

- Speeding up boilerplate code writing
- Learning new APIs with example snippets
- Enhancing code quality with AI hints

5.3 Codeium: Free AI Coding Assistant

Website: https://codeium.com

Codeium is a free AI assistant that supports code completion, code search, and refactoring suggestions across many languages. It integrates with popular editors and aims to democratize AI coding assistance.

Key Features

- Real-time AI code completions
- Multi-language support including Python, JavaScript, C++, and more
- Code search powered by AI understanding
- Free with no signup required

Use Cases

- General coding productivity boost
- Refactoring legacy code
- Discovering relevant code examples quickly

5.4 OpenDevin: Auto-Code & Execute

Repository: https://github.com/ibm/OpenDevin

OpenDevin is an IBM open-source project that enables automated code generation and execution. It combines AI coding capabilities with the ability to run and test generated code snippets dynamically.

Key Features

- Auto-generation of code snippets
- Automated code execution and result retrieval
- Integration with Jupyter notebooks and development workflows

Use Cases

- Rapid prototyping of algorithms
- Experimenting with code snippets and outputs in real-time

- Teaching programming concepts interactively

5.5 Cursor: AI-Native Coding IDE

Website: https://cursor.sh

Cursor is an AI-native IDE designed from the ground up to leverage AI assistance deeply in coding workflows. It provides intelligent code completions, code navigation, and refactoring tools embedded seamlessly within the development environment.

Key Features

- Smart code completions and suggestions
- AI-assisted code navigation and understanding
- Integrated debugging support
- Collaborative coding features

Use Cases

- Complex software development projects
- Codebase understanding and maintenance
- Pair programming with AI assistance

5.6 Replit Ghostwriter: Online IDE with AI (Free Tier Available)

Website: https://replit.com

Replit Ghostwriter is an AI-powered assistant embedded into the popular cloud-based IDE Replit. It supports coding in the browser, making it accessible on any device with features like AI code completions, error fixes, and explanations.

Key Features

- Cloud-based coding environment
- AI-driven code suggestions and completions
- Real-time collaboration and multiplayer coding
- Free tier with basic AI features

Use Cases

- Learning programming without setup
- Collaborative coding sessions
- Quick prototyping and sharing code online

5.7 Summary Table of AI Coding and Development Tools

Tool	Description	Link
GitHub Copilot	AI code completion (free for students)	github.com/features/copilot
Codeium	Free AI coding assistant	codeium.com
OpenDevin	Auto-code & execute	github.com/ibm/OpenDevin
Cursor	AI-native coding IDE	cursor.sh
Replit Ghostwriter	Online IDE with AI (free tier)	replit.com

table 7 : AI Coding and Development Tools

5.8 How to Get Started

1. **Choose your coding environment:** Decide between local IDE plugins (GitHub Copilot, Codeium, Cursor) or cloud IDEs (Replit Ghostwriter).
2. **Install or sign up:** Follow installation instructions or sign up for online platforms.
3. **Experiment with AI suggestions:** Write code as usual and observe AI completions or generate snippets.
4. **Validate AI-generated code:** Always review and test AI-suggested code for correctness and security.
5. **Explore advanced features:** Use debugging, refactoring, and collaborative tools to boost workflow.

5.9 Future Outlook

AI assistants for coding will become more integrated, understanding not only syntax but also project architecture, style preferences, and real-time feedback. Expect deeper collaboration between human developers and AI, automating larger portions of software development cycles.

5.10 Tutorials for Each Tool

5.10.1 GitHub Copilot Quick Start

1. Install the GitHub Copilot extension for your code editor (e.g., VS Code).
2. Sign in with your GitHub account and activate the free student plan if eligible.
3. Open a code file and start typing; Copilot will automatically suggest completions and snippets.
4. Use Tab or Ctrl+Space to accept suggestions.
5. Experiment with comments to generate code, e.g., write // function to reverse a string and Copilot suggests implementation.

5.10.2 Codcium Setup and Usage

1. Visit codeium.com and install the plugin for your IDE or editor.
2. No signup is required; enable the plugin after installation.
3. Start typing code and observe inline AI completions and suggestions.
4. Use shortcuts (configurable) to accept or cycle through suggestions.

5.10.3 OpenDevin Basic Usage

1. Clone the OpenDevin GitHub repo.
2. Follow setup instructions to install dependencies and configure runtime environment.
3. Use provided Jupyter notebook examples to generate and execute code snippets automatically.
4. Modify inputs to experiment with different programming tasks and see live results.

5.10.4 Cursor IDE Walkthrough

1. Sign up or install Cursor from cursor.sh.
2. Open or create a new project inside Cursor.
3. Type code to receive AI completions and utilize advanced navigation features.
4. Use integrated debugging tools enhanced by AI insights.
5. Collaborate with teammates using built-in sharing features.

5.10.5 Replit Ghostwriter Usage

1. Create a free account at replit.com.
2. Start a new repl (project) in your preferred programming language.
3. Enable Ghostwriter AI features from the sidebar.

4. Write code and receive AI-driven completions, fixes, and explanations.
5. Collaborate in real-time with others on the same repl.

5.11 Comparison Matrix: Pros, Cons, and Ideal Users

Tool	Pros	Cons	Ideal Users
GitHub Copilot	Powerful completions; integrates with popular IDEs; free for students	Paid subscription for general users	Students, professional developers
Codeium	Free, no signup; multi-language support	Less mature ecosystem than Copilot	Hobbyists, developers on budget
OpenDevin	Auto-code plus execution; open source	Requires setup and Python knowledge	Researchers, educators, prototypers
Cursor	AI-native IDE with rich features	Newer product, smaller user base	Professional dev teams, complex projects
Replit Ghostwriter	Cloud-based, collaboration, free tier available	Limited offline use; free tier has usage limits	Learners, remote teams, quick prototyping

table 8 : Matrix: Pros, Cons, and Ideal Users

5.12 Sample Project Ideas

- **GitHub Copilot:** Develop a REST API backend quickly by letting Copilot generate route handlers and data models.
- **Codeium:** Refactor an old codebase by using AI suggestions to improve readability and modularity.
- **OpenDevin:** Build a notebook that generates and tests sorting algorithms automatically.
- **Cursor:** Manage a large codebase by navigating and refactoring with AI-powered insights.
- **Replit Ghostwriter:** Create a multiplayer game prototype collaboratively with real-time AI code help.

5.13 Template Code Snippets

GitHub Copilot Example (Python function to check palindrome)

```python
python
CopyEdit
def is_palindrome(s: str) -> bool:
    # Check if the string is a palindrome
    return s == s[::-1]
```

(Copilot can generate this automatically when you write the comment.)

Codeium Example (JavaScript code completion)

```javascript
javascript
CopyEdit
// Function to fetch user data from API
async function fetchUserData(userId) {
    const response = await fetch(`/api/users/${userId}`);
    const data = await response.json();
    return data;
}
```

OpenDevin Example (Python snippet for Fibonacci sequence)

```python
python
CopyEdit
def fibonacci(n):
    if n <= 1:
        return n
    else:
        return fibonacci(n-1) + fibonacci(n-2)
print(fibonacci(10))
```

5.14 Best Practices for AI Coding Tools

1. **Review AI-generated code:** Always verify and test AI suggestions to avoid bugs or vulnerabilities.
2. **Use AI to complement, not replace:** AI accelerates development but human insight is critical.
3. **Protect sensitive code:** Be cautious about sharing proprietary or sensitive code with cloud-based AI services.

4. **Keep dependencies updated:** Use the latest stable versions of AI plugins and IDEs.
5. **Leverage AI for learning:** Use explanations and generated examples to understand new programming concepts.
6. **Maintain coding standards:** Ensure AI-generated code follows your project's style guides and best practices.

Chapter 6: AI for App and Game Creation

Creating apps and games has traditionally required extensive coding, design, and storytelling skills. AI-powered platforms and tools are now democratizing this process, enabling creators to build apps and games faster, generate stunning assets, and craft immersive narratives without deep technical expertise.

This chapter covers key AI-driven platforms across three major categories:

- Game creation platforms
- Game asset generation tools
- Narrative and dialogue AI systems

6.1 Introduction

App and game development involve multiple complex workflows: coding mechanics, designing visuals, and writing engaging stories. AI accelerates these steps by automating programming tasks, generating realistic assets, and simulating intelligent characters.

We review the top AI platforms that empower creators to bring their ideas to life more easily and creatively.

6.2 Game Creation Platforms

Platform	Description	Link
AppCreator24	Low-code/no-code app & game builder	appcreator24.com
Natively.dev	Cross-platform app/game builder with AI tools	natively.dev
GDevelop	Open-source, no-code game engine	gdevelop.io
Construct 3	Browser-based 2D game engine (Free tier available)	construct.net
Scratch	Visual block-based programming for beginners	scratch.mit.edu

table 9 : Game Creation Platforms

Highlights:

- These platforms enable app and game creation with little to no coding.
- GDevelop and Construct 3 are popular for 2D game development with active communities.
- Scratch is ideal for beginners and educational contexts.

6.3 Game Asset Generation Tools

Tool	Description	Link
Leonardo.Ai	AI-driven image generation focused on game assets	leonardo.ai
Scenario.gg	AI platform specialized in game asset creation	scenario.gg
Artbreeder	Collaborative AI tool for creating characters and art	artbreeder.com
This Person Does Not Exist	AI-generated realistic human faces	thispersondoesnotexist.com
Luma AI	3D scene capture and asset creation with AI	lumalabs.ai

table 10 : Game Asset Generation Tools

Highlights:

- Use these tools to generate characters, backgrounds, textures, and other game assets.
- Leonardo.Ai and Scenario.gg focus on fast, customizable game asset pipelines.
- Artbreeder offers creative blending and mutation of images.
- Luma AI adds 3D scanning capabilities using AI for immersive assets.

6.4 Narrative & Dialogue AI Tools

Tool	Description	Link
Inworld AI	AI-driven character simulation and dialogue	inworld.ai
Charisma.ai	Interactive storytelling and dialogue platform	charisma.ai
AI Dungeon	AI-generated text-based adventure and story creation	play.aidungeon.io
NovelAI	AI-assisted creative writing tool (trial available)	novelai.net

table 11 : Narrative & Dialogue AI Tools

Highlights:

- These platforms help create dynamic, immersive narratives and realistic character dialogues.
- Useful for games with strong story or role-playing elements.
- AI Dungeon and NovelAI specialize in interactive storytelling.

6.5 Summary Table of App and Game Creation Tools

Category	Tool/Platform	Description	Link
Game Creation	AppCreator24	No-code app & game builder	appcreator24.com
	Natively.dev	Cross-platform app/game builder	natively.dev
	GDevelop	Open-source 2D game engine	gdevelop.io
	Construct 3	Browser-based 2D game engine	construct.net
	Scratch	Visual programming for beginners	scratch.mit.edu
Asset Generation	Leonardo.Ai	AI game asset image generation	leonardo.ai
	Scenario.gg	AI game asset creation platform	scenario.gg
	Artbreeder	AI collaborative character art	artbreeder.com
	This Person Does Not Exist	AI-generated faces	thispersondoesnotexist.com
	Luma AI	3D scene capture & asset creation	lumalabs.ai
Narrative & Dialogue	Inworld AI	AI character simulation & dialogue	inworld.ai
	Charisma.ai	Interactive storytelling platform	charisma.ai
	AI Dungeon	AI-generated text adventure	play.aidungeon.io
	NovelAI	AI-assisted creative writing	novelai.net

table 12 : App and Game Creation Tools

6.6 How to Get Started

- Choose your focus area: game/app mechanics, asset creation, or narrative/dialogue.
- Start with no-code platforms like AppCreator24 or GDevelop for building basic games or apps.
- Use asset generation tools to quickly create characters, backgrounds, and textures.
- Integrate narrative AI to enrich game storytelling or dialogue systems.
- Prototype iteratively, combining tools to streamline the creative pipeline.

6.7 Tutorials for Key Platforms

6.7.1 Building a Simple Game with GDevelop

1. Visit gdevelop.io and create a free account.
2. Start a new project using a template or blank scene.
3. Use drag-and-drop events to add game logic without coding.
4. Import assets generated via Leonardo.Ai or Artbreeder for characters and backgrounds.
5. Test your game live in the browser and export to web or mobile.

6.7.2 Generating Game Characters with Artbreeder

1. Go to artbreeder.com and create a free account.
2. Choose "Create" and start with existing portraits or landscapes.
3. Adjust genes sliders to mutate features and combine styles.
4. Download high-resolution images for use as character sprites or concept art.

6.7.3 Creating Interactive Dialogue with Inworld AI

1. Sign up at inworld.ai.
2. Create a new character, customizing personality and speech patterns.
3. Integrate the character into your game or app via SDKs or APIs.
4. Use the dialogue editor to script possible interactions and responses.
5. Test conversations with the AI character in real-time.

6.7.4 Prototyping with Construct 3 (Free Tier)

1. Access construct.net and create a free account.
2. Use visual event sheets to add game mechanics like player movement or scoring.
3. Incorporate AI-generated assets from Scenario.gg or This Person Does Not Exist.
4. Preview the game instantly in your browser and share with others.

6.7.5 Writing Game Storylines with NovelAI

1. Visit novelai.net and sign up for a trial.
2. Start a new story project and input basic plot or character ideas.
3. Use AI to generate descriptive text, dialogue, or branching narrative paths.
4. Export generated text for integration into your game's story or quest design.

6.8 Comparison Matrix: Pros, Cons, and Ideal Users

Tool/Platform	Pros	Cons	Ideal Users
AppCreator24	No-code app/game building; fast prototyping	Limited customization beyond templates	Beginners, hobbyists, rapid app creators
Natively.dev	Cross-platform deployment; AI tools	Requires some technical familiarity	Indie devs, cross-platform app creators
GDevelop	Open-source, community support, no coding	Less suited for 3D games	Educators, indie developers, beginners
Construct 3	Browser-based, visual scripting, free tier	Paid tiers for advanced features	Educators, hobbyists, 2D game developers
Scratch	Visual programming for kids and beginners	Limited complexity for commercial games	Educators, kids, absolute beginners
Leonardo.Ai	Fast, customizable game asset generation	Still maturing; asset licensing considerations	Artists, game devs needing assets quickly
Scenario.gg	AI asset pipelines optimized for games	Requires subscription for high-quality assets	Game studios, professional artists
Artbreeder	Unique blending and creation of art	Limited to 2D images and concepts	Character designers, artists
This Person Does Not Exist	Realistic human faces generation	Limited control over generated features	Game devs needing realistic NPC portraits
Luma AI	AI-driven 3D scene capture and reconstruction	Requires hardware for scanning; early stage	3D artists, AR/VR developers
Inworld AI	Rich character simulation and dialogue	SDK integration needed; pricing varies	Narrative designers, RPG/game developers
Charisma.ai	Interactive storytelling platform	Subscription-based pricing	Storytellers, interactive media creators
AI Dungeon	Dynamic story generation, easy to use	Story quality varies; online only	Writers, gamers, interactive fiction fans

NovelAI	Creative writing with AI assistance	Paid service with trial only	Authors, game writers, narrative designers

table 13 : Comparison Matrix: Pros, Cons, and Ideal Users

6.9 Sample Project Ideas

- **Create a simple platformer game in GDevelop using AI-generated characters and backgrounds from Leonardo.Ai.**
- **Build an interactive NPC with rich dialogue using Inworld AI for a role-playing game.**
- **Design a branching storyline with NovelAI and integrate it into a Construct 3 game.**
- **Generate multiple realistic character portraits with This Person Does Not Exist for use as game avatars.**
- **Prototype a mobile app using AppCreator24 incorporating AI-generated UI assets from Scenario.gg.**

6.10 Best Practices for AI-Driven App and Game Creation

1. **Plan your creative pipeline:** Decide early how AI tools fit into design, asset creation, and storytelling phases.
2. **Maintain artistic control:** Use AI to augment creativity, not replace your vision. Edit and refine AI-generated assets carefully.
3. **Check licensing:** Verify terms of use and licenses for AI-generated assets before commercial use.
4. **Prototype iteratively:** Combine no-code game engines with AI assets and narrative tools for rapid testing.
5. **Optimize for platform:** Ensure AI-generated assets and scripts are suitable for your target device (mobile, desktop, web).
6. **Test player experience:** Make sure AI-driven narratives and dialogues feel natural and engaging through playtesting.
7. **Backup work frequently:** AI tools and platforms are evolving; save versions and exports regularly to avoid data loss.

Chapter 7: AI for Design, Art, and Media

AI is revolutionizing creative fields like design, digital art, and media production by enabling the rapid generation of images, stylized artwork, and multimedia content. AI-powered text-to-image tools, stylization apps, and experimental open-source projects empower creators to explore new visual styles, produce high-quality art, and streamline their workflows.

This chapter explores a diverse selection of AI tools transforming art and media creation.

7.1 Introduction

The integration of AI in design and art has unlocked powerful new ways to create visual content. From generating images based on simple text prompts to applying artistic styles to photos, AI tools help both professionals and hobbyists push creative boundaries.

This chapter categorizes these tools into:

- Text-to-Image generation
- Stylized and artistic apps
- Mobile AI art apps
- Experimental and open-source projects

7.2 Text-to-Image Tools

Tool	Description	Link
Craiyon	Free, easy text-to-image generation	craiyon.com
Bing Image Creator	Microsoft-powered AI image generator	bing.com/images/create
Playground AI	Advanced AI image generation platform	playgroundai.com
NightCafe Studio	AI art generation with styles & community	nightcafe.studio
Mage.space	AI art generation with customization	mage.space

table 14 : Text-to-Image Tools

Highlights:

- Generate images from text prompts with ease.
- Each platform offers different style presets and controls.
- Some provide community galleries and sharing features.

7.3 Stylized & Artistic Tools

Tool	Description	Link
Deep Dream Generator	AI-driven surreal and dream-like art	deepdreamgenerator.com
WOMBO Dream	AI art creation with vivid styles	dream.ai
StarryAI	AI art generation focusing on creativity	starryai.com

table 15 : Stylized & Artistic Tools

Highlights:

- Focus on creating unique, stylized artistic images.
- Some tools enable guided style transfer and user control.
- Often support high-resolution downloads and print-ready outputs.

7.4 Mobile AI Art Apps

App	Description	Platforms
Dream by Wombo	AI-powered art generation on mobile	Android, iOS
Imagine AI Art Generator	Mobile app for instant AI art creation	Android, iOS
AI Mirror	AI art and photo stylization	Android, iOS

Highlights:

- Create art on the go with mobile-friendly interfaces.
- Combine photo stylization and text-to-image capabilities.
- Easy sharing on social media platforms.

7.5 Experimental and Open Source Projects

Project	Description	Link
Hugging Face Diffusers	Open-source diffusion models for image generation	huggingface.co/spaces
InvokeAI	Community-driven open-source Stable Diffusion fork	invoke.ai
Stable Diffusion Web UI	Web interface for running Stable Diffusion locally or remotely	github.com

table 16 : Experimental and Open Source Projects

Highlights:

- Highly customizable and privacy-focused options.
- Run AI art generation on local machines or private servers.
- Strong communities and continuous improvements.

7.6 Summary Table of Design, Art, and Media Tools

Category	Tool/App	Description	Link
Text-to-Image	Craiyon	Free text-to-image generation	craiyon.com
	Bing Image Creator	Microsoft AI image generation	bing.com/images/create
	Playground AI	Advanced image generation platform	playgroundai.com
	NightCafe Studio	AI art with style options	nightcafe.studio
	Mage.space	Customizable AI art generator	mage.space
Stylized & Artistic	Deep Dream Generator	Surreal, dream-like AI art	deepdreamgenerator.com
	WOMBO Dream	Vivid AI art styles	dream.ai
	StarryAI	Creative AI art generation	starryai.com
Mobile Apps	Dream by Wombo	Mobile AI art generation	Android/iOS
	Imagine AI Art Generator	Mobile instant AI art creation	Android/iOS
	AI Mirror	AI photo stylization	Android/iOS
Open Source/Experimental	Hugging Face Diffusers	Open-source diffusion model space	huggingface.co/spaces
	InvokeAI	Open-source Stable Diffusion fork	invoke.ai
	Stable Diffusion Web UI	Web interface for Stable Diffusion	github.com

table 17 : Design, Art, and Media Tools

7.7 How to Get Started

- Select a tool matching your skill level and device (web, desktop, or mobile).
- Experiment with simple text prompts to generate images or apply styles.
- Use open-source tools if you want local control and customization.
- Combine text-to-image tools with stylization apps for unique creative outputs.
- Share your creations on community galleries or social media to get feedback.

7.8 Tutorials for Popular Tools

7.8.1 Using Craiyon for Text-to-Image Generation

1. Go to craiyon.com.
2. Enter a descriptive text prompt (e.g., "sunset over mountains in impressionist style").
3. Click **Draw** and wait for the AI to generate images.
4. Browse through generated results, click to enlarge, and download desired images.
5. Experiment with prompt variations to refine results.

7.8.2 Creating Stylized Art with Deep Dream Generator

1. Visit deepdreamgenerator.com.
2. Upload a photo or choose from gallery images.
3. Select an artistic style preset or upload your own style image.
4. Generate the dream-like styled output.
5. Save or share your artwork on social platforms.

7.8.3 Generating Mobile AI Art with Dream by Wombo

1. Download Dream by Wombo on Android or iOS.
2. Open the app and enter a text prompt describing your desired image.
3. Choose an art style from the available options.
4. Generate artwork and save or share it directly from the app.

7.8.4 Running Stable Diffusion Locally with Stable Diffusion Web UI

1. Visit the GitHub repo.
2. Follow detailed installation instructions to set up the environment (Python, dependencies).
3. Run the Web UI locally on your machine.
4. Enter prompts, adjust parameters (steps, CFG scale), and generate images.
5. Explore extensions and plugins for enhanced features.

7.9 Comparison Matrix: Pros, Cons, and Ideal Users

Tool/Category	Pros	Cons	Ideal Users
Craiyon	Free and accessible; easy to use	Lower image resolution and quality	Beginners, casual creators
Bing Image Creator	Powered by Microsoft; good image variety	Requires Microsoft account; limited customization	General users, Microsoft ecosystem users
Playground AI	Advanced controls and styles	Some features behind paywall	Hobbyists and professional creators
NightCafe Studio	Community features; high-quality styles	Paid credits needed for high-res outputs	Artists, social creators
Mage.space	Customizable AI generation	UI less polished	Creative professionals
Deep Dream Generator	Unique surreal effects; easy web access	Niche style; not for realistic images	Experimental artists
WOMBO Dream	Mobile-friendly; vivid art styles	Limited control over results	Mobile users, casual creators
StarryAI	Creative and unique styles	Somewhat niche use case	Digital artists
Dream by Wombo	On-the-go creation; user-friendly	Mobile-only; limited export options	Mobile creators
Hugging Face Diffusers	Open source and flexible	Requires technical skills	Developers, researchers
InvokeAI	Strong community and support	Setup complexity	AI enthusiasts, advanced users
Stable Diffusion Web UI	Powerful local generation with plugins	Setup can be complex	Developers, power users

table 18: Comparison Matrix: Pros, Cons, and Ideal Users

7.10 Sample Project Ideas

- Create a series of surreal artworks using Deep Dream Generator and post a themed gallery online.
- Use Playground AI to generate a set of concept art for a graphic novel.
- Develop a mobile wallpaper app using AI art generated from Dream by Wombo.
- Run Stable Diffusion Web UI locally to generate background images for a game or website.
- Collaborate in online communities by sharing and iterating AI-generated images.

7.11 Best Practices for AI in Design and Media

1. **Be clear with prompts:** The more descriptive your text input, the better the AI results.
2. **Combine tools:** Use multiple AI tools for generation and stylization to create unique effects.
3. **Respect copyright:** Verify usage rights for AI-generated images, especially for commercial use.
4. **Keep human creativity central:** AI is a tool to augment, not replace, artistic vision.
5. **Experiment often:** AI models respond to creative experimentation—try varied styles and inputs.
6. **Share and get feedback:** Use community features to improve your craft and discover trends.
7. **Optimize outputs:** Resize and retouch AI images as needed for your projects.

Chapter 8: Summary Table of All Free AI Tools

This chapter provides a comprehensive summary table listing all the free AI tools introduced in the previous chapters. It serves as a handy reference guide for selecting the right AI tool for your needs, whether for research, productivity, coding, game development, or creative art.

8.1 Summary Table: Free AI Tools by Category

Category	Tool/Platform	Description	Link
AI for Learning & Research	Elicit	Literature review, summary extraction	elicit.org
	Perplexity AI	Real-time research with citations	perplexity.ai
	Consensus	Peer-reviewed answers to questions	consensus.app
	Scite Assistant	Analyze & explain scientific papers	scite.ai
	ResearchRabbit	Visualize paper networks & discovery	researchrabbit.ai
AI for Productivity & Personal Use	Pi (Inflection AI)	Emotional AI assistant	pi.ai
	ChatGPT Free	General-purpose assistant	chat.openai.com
	Notion AI (limited free)	AI inside Notion workspace	notion.so
	Mem.ai	Smart AI note-taking	mem.ai
	Taskade AI	Task management & mind maps	taskade.com
Autonomous Agents & Task Automation	AgentGPT	Create autonomous agents	agentgpt.reworkd.ai
	Auto-GPT	Python-based autonomous agent	GitHub
	BabyAGI	Task queue AI	GitHub

		agent	
	Runner AI	No-code AI automation	runner.hcompany.ai
	Zapier AI	Automate app workflows	zapier.com/ai
AI for Coding & Development	GitHub Copilot (Free for students)	AI code completion	github.com/features/copilot
	Codeium	Free AI coding assistant	codeium.com
	OpenDevin	Auto-code & execute	GitHub
	Cursor	AI-native coding IDE	cursor.sh
	Replit Ghostwriter (Free tier)	Online IDE with AI	replit.com
AI for App & Game Creation	AppCreator24	No-code app & game builder	appcreator24.com
	Natively.dev	Cross-platform app/game builder	natively.dev
	GDevelop	Open-source 2D game engine	gdevelop.io
	Construct 3 (Free tier)	Browser-based 2D game engine	construct.net
	Scratch	Visual block-based programming for beginners	scratch.mit.edu
	Leonardo.Ai	AI game asset image generation	leonardo.ai
	Scenario.gg	AI game asset creation platform	scenario.gg
	Artbreeder	AI collaborative character art	artbreeder.com

	This Person Does Not Exist	AI-generated realistic human faces	thispersondoesnotexist.com
	Luma AI	3D scene capture & asset creation	lumalabs.ai
	Inworld AI	AI character simulation & dialogue	inworld.ai
	Charisma.ai	Interactive storytelling platform	charisma.ai
	AI Dungeon	AI-generated text adventure	play.aidungeon.io
	NovelAI (trial)	AI-assisted creative writing	novelai.net
AI for Design, Art & Media	Craiyon	Free text-to-image generation	craiyon.com
	Bing Image Creator	Microsoft AI image generation	bing.com/images/create
	Playground AI	Advanced image generation platform	playgroundai.com
	NightCafe Studio	AI art generation with styles & community	nightcafe.studio
	Mage.space	Customizable AI art generator	mage.space
	Deep Dream Generator	Surreal, dream-like AI art	deepdreamgenerator.com
	WOMBO Dream	AI art creation with vivid styles	dream.ai
	StarryAI	Creative AI art generation	starryai.com

	Dream by Wombo	Mobile AI art generation	Android/iOS
	Imagine AI Art Generator	Mobile instant AI art creation	Android/iOS
	AI Mirror	AI art and photo stylization	Android/iOS
	Hugging Face Diffusers	Open-source diffusion models for image generation	huggingface.co/spaces
	InvokeAI	Community open-source Stable Diffusion fork	invoke.ai
	Stable Diffusion Web UI	Web interface for running Stable Diffusion locally	github.com

table 19: Free AI Tools by Category

8.2 How to Use This Table

- Identify your category of interest (e.g., coding, productivity, design).
- Browse the tools and platforms listed along with descriptions.
- Visit the provided links to explore, sign up, or download the tools.
- Consider tutorials in previous chapters for guided onboarding.
- Experiment with multiple tools to find the best fit for your workflow.

8.3 Tips for Choosing Free AI Tools

- **Check limitations:** Some free tiers may have usage caps or limited features.
- **Privacy considerations:** Verify data handling and privacy policies, especially for sensitive work.
- **Community and support:** Opt for tools with active communities or good documentation.
- **Integration:** Ensure the tool fits into your existing workflow or platform (IDE, web, mobile).

- **Purpose-fit:** Select tools aligned with your specific goals — research, coding, creative work, etc.

8.4 Final Thoughts

Free AI tools have dramatically lowered the barrier to entry for leveraging artificial intelligence across many domains. With a little exploration and practice, users ranging from students to professionals can harness these tools to improve productivity, creativity, and innovation.

Keep this chapter handy as a quick reference to stay updated with the best free AI tools available today.

General Conclusion

Artificial Intelligence is no longer a distant promise—it is a living, evolving reality that is reshaping the way we learn, teach, and conduct research. For students and researchers alike, the academic journey has traditionally involved long hours of reading, writing, organizing data, and searching for relevant sources. Today, with the support of AI tools, much of this cognitive and logistical burden can be eased—if not transformed.

Throughout this guide, we have explored a variety of tools—some designed to generate ideas, others to synthesize vast volumes of literature, analyze data, assist with writing, or even offer personalized learning recommendations. Each of these tools represents a shift in how knowledge can be accessed, processed, and communicated. They are not mere technical utilities—they are, in many ways, intellectual partners in the academic process.

But with great power comes great responsibility. As we adopt these tools, we must do so critically. AI should not replace the human capacity for thought, reflection, or ethical judgment. It should amplify it. This requires developing a form of **AI literacy**—the ability to understand how these tools work, when to trust them, and when to question them. It also means fostering academic integrity by being transparent about the use of AI and resisting the temptation to rely on it as a shortcut.

Let us not forget that the core of research is curiosity, creativity, and a desire to contribute something meaningful to the world. AI can accelerate the process, but it cannot replace the spark that drives inquiry. Nor can it substitute the nuanced understanding that comes from years of study, collaboration, and critical engagement.

Moreover, the accessibility of AI tools offers a unique opportunity to democratize knowledge production. Students and researchers in under-resourced environments now have access to powerful tools that were once limited to elite institutions. This shift holds the potential to bridge gaps in access, elevate underrepresented voices, and foster more inclusive academic ecosystems.

Looking ahead, the future of research and education will be marked by collaboration—not only among people but also between humans and machines. Embracing this new paradigm requires openness, adaptability, and a willingness to continuously learn—not just about our subjects, but also about the technologies that shape our work.

In closing, this guide is not an endpoint but a beginning. It is an invitation to explore, experiment, and engage with the AI tools that are now part of our academic lives. May you use them wisely, creatively, and ethically—as tools not of replacement, but of enhancement. The future of learning and research is in your hands—and your mind, empowered by intelligent systems, is more capable than ever before.

References

1. Boudry, M., & Heesen, R. (2023). *Should we trust AI to write academic texts?* Trends in Cognitive Sciences, 27(2), 87–89. https://doi.org/10.1016/j.tics.2022.11.001
2. Alshater, M. M. (2023). *Exploring the role of ChatGPT in academic writing: Advantages, limitations, and ethical considerations*. Journal of Applied Research in Higher Education. https://doi.org/10.1108/JARHE-02-2023-0063
3. Lund, B. D., Wang, T., Mannix, T., & Berne, J. (2023). *Generative AI and ChatGPT in education: A cautionary view*. International Journal of Educational Technology in Higher Education, 20(1), 1–9. https://doi.org/10.1186/s41239-023-00371-9
4. Tlili, A., Wang, X., Huang, R., et al. (2023). *What if the devil is my guardian angel: ChatGPT as a case study of using chatbots in education*. Smart Learning Environments, 10(15). https://doi.org/10.1186/s40561-023-00237-3
5. Gilson, A., Safranek, C. W., Huang, T. K., et al. (2023). *How well does ChatGPT do when taking the medical licensing exams?* PLOS Digital Health, 2(2), e0000198. https://doi.org/10.1371/journal.pdig.0000198
6. Floridi, L., & Chiriatti, M. (2020). *GPT-3: Its nature, scope, limits, and consequences*. Minds and Machines, 30(4), 681–694. https://doi.org/10.1007/s11023-020-09548-1
7. O'Connor, S., & ChatGPT. (2023). *Open artificial intelligence platforms in nursing education: Tools for academic productivity or a threat to integrity?* Nurse Education in Practice, 64, 103511. https://doi.org/10.1016/j.nepr.2023.103511
8. Dwivedi, Y. K., Hughes, D. L., Ismagilova, E., et al. (2021). *Artificial Intelligence (AI): Multidisciplinary perspectives on emerging challenges, opportunities, and agenda for research, practice and policy*. International Journal of Information Management, 57, 101994. https://doi.org/10.1016/j.ijinfomgt.2019.08.002
9. King, M. R., & ChatGPT. (2023). *A conversation on artificial intelligence, ChatGPT, and scholarly publishing*. The American Journal of Medicine, 136(4), 303–304. https://doi.org/10.1016/j.amjmed.2023.01.011
10. van Dis, E. A. M., Bollen, J., Zuidema, W., van Rooij, R., & Bockting, C. L. H. (2023). *ChatGPT: Five priorities for research*. Nature, 614(7947), 224–226. https://doi.org/10.1038/d41586-023-00288-7
11. Kasneci, E., Sessler, K., & Kasneci, G. (2023). *ChatGPT for good? On opportunities and challenges of large language models for education*. Learning and Individual Differences, 103, 102274. https://doi.org/10.1016/j.lindif.2023.102274

12. Yuan, T., & Zhou, Y. (2023). *The use of AI in academic research: A systematic review.* Journal of Scholarly Publishing, 54(3), 165–183. https://doi.org/10.3138/jsp-2023-0011
13. Jwa, H., Qi, P., Li, Y., & Jurafsky, D. (2019). *Authorship attribution in academic writing using deep learning*. Transactions of the Association for Computational Linguistics, 7, 219–232. https://doi.org/10.1162/tacl_a_00270
14. Zhai, X. (2022). *ChatGPT and AI-generated content: The next wave of plagiarism in academic publishing?* Journal of Academic Ethics, 21(3), 231–237. https://doi.org/10.1007/s10805-022-09412-8
15. Esteva, A., Robicquet, A., Ramsundar, B., et al. (2019). *A guide to deep learning in healthcare*. Nature Medicine, 25(1), 24–29. https://doi.org/10.1038/s41591-018-0316-z
16. McGee, P. (2023). *AI and academic writing: Friend or foe?* Teaching in Higher Education, 28(1), 1–4. https://doi.org/10.1080/13562517.2023.2178783
17. Gao, C. A., Howard, F. M., Markov, N. S., et al. (2022). *Comparing scientific abstracts generated by ChatGPT to original abstracts using an artificial intelligence output detector, plagiarism detector, and blinded human reviewers*. bioRxiv. https://doi.org/10.1101/2022.12.23.521610
18. Lajoie, S. P. (2020). *Emerging roles for AI in education: Current applications and future directions*. AI in Education, 12163, 5–13. https://doi.org/10.1007/978-3-030-52237-7_1
19. Sadiq, M. W., & Ventura, D. (2023). *Ethical implications of using ChatGPT in education: A review*. Journal of Educational Technology & Society, 26(1), 45–56.
20. Marcus, G., & Davis, E. (2020). *GPT-3, Bloviator: OpenAI's language generator has no idea what it's talking about*. MIT Technology Review. https://www.technologyreview.com/2020/08/22/1007539/gpt3-openai-language-generator-artificial-intelligence-ai-opinion/
21. Walton, G., & Hepworth, M. (2021). *Developing AI literacy in higher education*. Journal of Information Literacy, 15(1), 20–35. https://doi.org/10.11645/15.1.2801
22. OpenAI. (2023). *ChatGPT and Education: Benefits and Limitations*. https://openai.com/blog/chatgpt-in-education/
23. Holmes, W., Bialik, M., & Fadel, C. (2019). *Artificial Intelligence in Education: Promises and Implications for Teaching and Learning*. Center for Curriculum Redesign. https://curriculumredesign.org/wp-content/uploads/AI-in-Education.pdf
24. World Economic Forum. (2023). *The Future of Jobs Report: How AI is Reshaping Work and Skills in Education and Research*. https://www.weforum.org/reports/the-future-of-jobs-report-2023/

25.UNESCO. (2021). *AI and Education: Guidance for Policy-makers*. https://unesdoc.unesco.org/ark:/48223/pf0000376709

FSC
www.fsc.org
MIX
Papier | Fördert gute Waldnutzung
FSC® C083411

Kolibri 360 GmbH
Ferdinand-Jühlke-Straße 7
99095 Erfurt, Deutschland
produktsicherheit@kolibri360.de

Druck:
CPI Druckdienstleistungen GmbH
im Auftrag der
Kolibri 360 GmbH
Ferdinand-Jühlke-Str. 7
99095 Erfurt